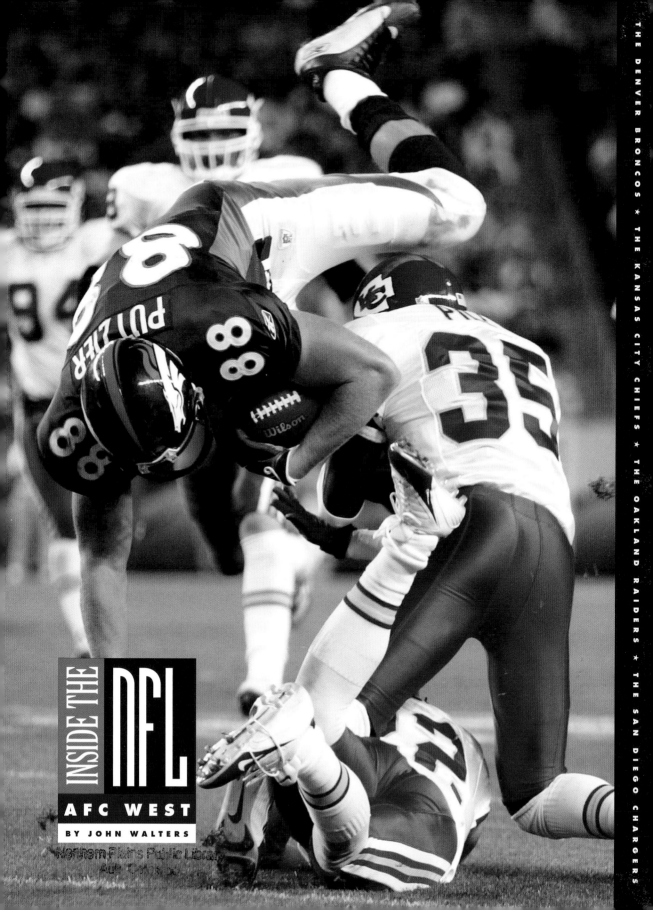

INSIDE THE NFL

AFC WEST

BY JOHN WALTERS

LIBRARY OF CONGRESS CATALOGING-IN-PUBLICATION DATA

Walters, John.
  AFC West / by John Walters.
    p. cm. – (Inside the NFL)
  Includes index.
  ISBN 1-59296-511-3 (library bound : alk. paper) 1. National Football
League–History–Juvenile literature. 2. Football–United States–History–Juvenile
literature. I. Title: American Football Conference West. II. Title. III. Child's World of
sports. Inside the NFL
  GV955.5.N35W664 2006
  796.332'64'0973–dc22   2005004811

ACKNOWLEDGEMENTS

The Child's World®: Mary Berendes, Publishing Director

Editorial Directions, Inc.: Russell Primm, Editorial Director and Line Editor; Matt
Messbarger, Project Editor; Elizabeth K. Martin, Assistant Editor; Olivia Nellums,
Editorial Assistant; Susan Hindman, Copy Editor; Susan Ashley, Beth Franken,
Proofreaders; Kevin Cunningham, Fact Checker; Tim Griffin/IndexServ, Indexer;
James Buckley Jr., Photo Researcher and Selector

The Design Lab: Kathleen Petelinsek, Design and Page Production

Photos: Cover: Denis Poroy/AP
Elise Amandola/AP: 12; AP: 11, 26, 27, 30; Brian Bahr/Getty:1; Bettmann/
Corbis: 8; Scott Boehm/Getty: 2; Stephen Dunn/Getty: 19, 21; Focus on Sport/
Getty: 28; Larry French/Getty: 14, 41; Jeff Gross/Getty: 23; Paul Spinelli/Getty:
32; Sports Gallery/Al Messerschmidt: 7, 10, 16, 18, 20, 25, 35, 36, 37; Rick
Stewart/Getty: 38.

AFC WEST

TABLE OF CONTENTS

Published in the United States of America by
The Child's World® • PO Box 326
Chanhassen, MN 55317-0326
800-599-READ• www.childsworld.com

The
Child's
World®

THE DENVER BRONCOS ★ THE KANSAS CITY CHIEFS ★ THE OAKLAND RAIDERS ★ THE SAN DIEGO CHARGERS

INTRODUCTION

DENVER BRONCOS

Year Founded: 1960

Home Stadium:
Invesco Field at Mile
High

Year Stadium
Opened: 2001

Team Colors:
Orange and blue

**KANSAS CITY
CHIEFS**

Year Founded: 1960

Home Stadium:
Arrowhead Stadium

Year Stadium
Opened: 1972

Team Colors: Red
and gold

The roots of the AFC (American Football Conference) West can be traced to 1958 and to future
Kansas City Chiefs owner Lamar Hunt. A wealthy
26-year-old Dallas businessman, Hunt hoped to
purchase the Chicago Cardinals (now the Arizona
Cardinals) and relocate them to Texas. The National
Football League (NFL) didn't let him, however. Hunt
then attempted to persuade the NFL to put an **expansion team** in Dallas (the Cowboys did not yet exist).
Again, he was denied. Frustrated, Hunt formed his
own league, the American Football League (AFL),
with seven other owners.

Hunt and his cohorts called themselves "The
Foolish Club" because other rival leagues to the NFL
had come and gone. But in 1960, the AFL began a
successful 10-year run. The four teams that today
make up the AFC West—the Denver Broncos, the
Kansas City Chiefs, the Oakland Raiders, and the

San Diego Chargers—were then the AFL's Western Conference, although you might not recognize those franchises today.

The San Diego Chargers were then the Los Angeles Chargers. The Kansas City Chiefs were the Dallas Texans. The Broncos played in Denver, but were outfitted in ugly brown-and-yellow uniforms with vertical-striped socks! The Oakland Raiders played across the San Francisco Bay in Kezar Stadium.

Thanks in part to the wild, wild AFL West, Hunt's league flourished. In 1970, the AFL West became the AFC West after the NFL-AFL merger formed the American and National Football Conferences. The Tampa Bay Buccaneers, an expansion team, joined the AFC West in 1976, but moved to the NFC Central the next year. The Seattle Seahawks joined the AFC West in 1977 and resided there until 2002, when the NFL realigned from six to eight divisions and Seattle migrated to the NFC West. The Raiders moved to Los Angeles from 1982 to 1994, but are now back in Oakland.

AFC West teams have been to the **Super Bowl** 13 times, winning six. More than that, though, this division has provided some of the most outrageous and incredible moments in pro football history. Inside, you'll read about the "Heidi Game," the NFL's longest game, the "Immaculate Reception," and "The Drive," just to name a few.

OAKLAND RAIDERS

Year Founded: 1960

Home Stadium: Network Associates Coliseum

Year Stadium Opened: 1966

Team Colors: Silver and black

SAN DIEGO CHARGERS

Year Founded: 1960

Home Stadium: Qualcomm Stadium

Year Stadium Opened: 1967

Team Colors: Blue and gold

CHAPTER ONE

THE DENVER BRONCOS

I f the Denver Broncos had any horseshoes for good luck, they were all pointed in the wrong direction in the franchise's early years. Denver won the first AFL game ever played, beating the Boston Patriots 13–10 on September 9, 1960. However, the Broncos would not have a winning season until 1973 and would not make the playoffs until 1977.

Denver began play in chocolate-colored jerseys with gold helmets and pants. They wore socks with vertical stripes. After going 4–9–1 and 3–11 their first two seasons, the Broncos fired coach Frank Filchock. The new coach, Jack Faulkner, destroyed Denver's striped socks at a public bonfire and ordered burnt-orange jerseys. The manufacturer delivered bright-orange jerseys by mistake.

Wearing bright orange, Denver finished in last place in the AFL West each of the next five years. In the 1966 season-opener, a 45–7 loss to the Houston Oilers, the Broncos failed to make a single first down. In 1968, Denver moved into newly enlarged

John Elway earned the nickname "Captain Comeback" by leading the Broncos on 47 come-from-behind, fourth-quarter drives during his career.

Running back Floyd Little was the Broncos' first star player.

and renamed Mile High Stadium, which would provide a huge home-field advantage over the next three decades. In 1970, halfback Floyd Little, the franchise's first **bona fide** star, led the AFC in rushing with 901 yards. Denver won four of its first five games that year but finished just 5–8–1. Their bad luck continued for another six years.

The Broncos' fortunes changed in 1977, however. Craig Morton, the 26th starting quarterback

Ed "Wahoo" McDaniel was a linebacker for the Broncos from 1961 to 1963. After his NFL playing career ended in 1968, he went on to greater fame as a professional wrestler.

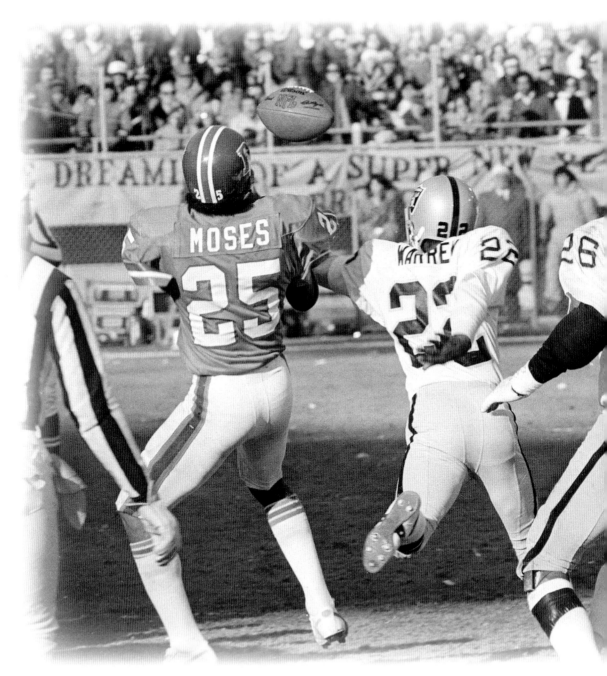

The Broncos reached the Super Bowl for the first time by
beating the Raiders in the 1977 AFC title game.

in franchise history, led Denver to a 12–2 season. Finally, the Broncos were in the playoffs. Denver's vaunted "Orange Crush" defense featured All-Pros Lyle Alzado, Rubin Carter, Randy Gradishar, and Tom Jackson.

On Christmas Eve at Mile High Stadium, the Broncos won their first playoff game, humbling the Pittsburgh Steelers, 34–21. A week later, the Broncos edged the defending Super Bowl-champion Oakland Raiders, 20–17, earning a berth in Super Bowl XII. Head coach Red Miller's team needed to play its best game to beat Dallas in the Super Bowl. Instead, the Broncos played their worst. Denver committed eight turnovers and lost 27–10.

In 1981, Dan Reeves was hired as head coach. Two years later, the Broncos made the biggest trade in franchise history when they acquired quarterback John Elway. The Stanford University quarterback had been made the number-one pick in the NFL draft by the Colts. Elway, the most publicized rookie since perhaps the Jets' Joe Namath in 1965, had good looks, nimble feet, and a rifle arm. He would be Denver's star for the next 16 years.

As great as Elway was—he is among the NFL's all-time best quarterbacks—he also holds the NFL record for most times sacked (516).

**Quarterback John Elway (7) and head coach Dan Reeves (right)
helped turn the Broncos into an AFC power.**

Terrell Davis, the
Most Valuable
Player (MVP) of
Super Bowl XXXII
and the 1998 league
MVP, was originally
selected in the sixth
round of the 1995
NFL draft.

Elway led the Broncos to the playoffs his first
two seasons. In his fourth year, he forged his legend
with what is now simply known as "The Drive."
Trailing 20–13 in frigid Cleveland in the AFC Championship Game, Elway marched the Broncos 98 yards
in the final minutes for the game-tying touchdown.
Denver won in overtime on Rich Karlis's field goal.

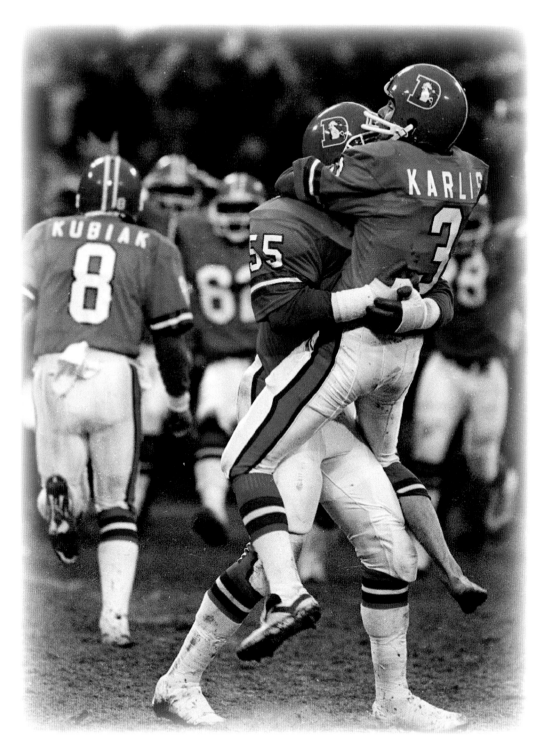

Rich Karlis (3) kicked the overtime field goal that won the 1986 AFC championship.

Running back Terrell Davis was the MVP of Denver's win over Green Bay in Super Bowl XXXII.

The Broncos met the New York Giants in Super Bowl XXI in Pasadena. Again, the Broncos failed to win the big game, losing 39–20. Unfortunately, a pattern was developing. The next year,

Denver won the AFC championship again, only to lose to the Washington Redskins in Super Bowl XXII in San Diego, 42–10.

Two years later, Denver was off to its fourth Super Bowl, this time against a San Francisco 49ers team that was clearly superior. The Broncos were buried, 55–10, in the most lopsided Super Bowl in history.

After a few average seasons, the Broncos returned to the Super Bowl in 1997 under third-year coach Mike Shanahan. Elway, finally teamed with a great running back in Terrell Davis and an All-Pro tight end in Shannon Sharpe, led the Broncos past the Green Bay Packers, 31–24, in Super Bowl XXXII.

The Broncos were back in the Super Bowl the following year. This time, they beat former coach Reeves and his Atlanta Falcons, 34–19. Elway, playing in his final game, was named MVP.

Since then, the Broncos haven't won a postseason game as they have searched for a worthy successor to Elway. Brian Griese, the son of Hall of Fame quarterback Bob Griese, was the first to fill Elway's shoes. But after Denver missed the playoffs three times in the four years immediately following Elway's retirement, the Broncos signed free-agent quarterback Jake Plummer in 2003. Plummer helped lead Denver to back-to-back 10-win seasons and a wild-card spot in the playoffs each of his first two seasons with the club.

Injuries forced Davis into retirement, too, so the Broncos turned to Clinton Portis in 2002. He had one of the NFL's best rookie seasons ever in 2002, running for 1,508 yards, then added 1,591 yards the

Denver's Mike Anderson set an NFL rookie record by rushing for 256 yards in a game against the Saints in 2000.

Quarterback Jake Plummer led the Broncos to back-to-back playoff berths in 2003 and 2004.

With 108 victories through the 2004 season, Mike Shanahan trails only Dan Reeves (117) among all-time Broncos coaches.

next year. But Denver, desperate for help on the defensive side of the ball, traded him to Washington for star cornerback Champ Bailey before the 2004 season.

In the end, though, it didn't help. The Broncos suffered the same fate in 2004—a blowout loss to Indianapolis in the wild-card round of the playoffs—that they did in 2003.

CHAPTER TWO

THE KANSAS CITY CHIEFS

"**B**efore there was a player, coach, or general manager in the AFL, there was Lamar Hunt," former Patriots owner Billy Sullivan once said. "Hunt was the **cornerstone** of the league."

If Lamar Hunt is the father of the AFL, the Kansas City Chiefs were the league's first-born. They were originally the Dallas Texans, sharing the Cotton Bowl with the NFL-expansion Dallas Cowboys in 1960.

After second-place finishes in each of their first two seasons, the Texans signed quarterback Len Dawson, an NFL castoff, in 1962. Dawson led the Texans to an 11–3 record. They capped the season with a 20–17 victory over the Houston Oilers in the AFL Championship Game. The game was a classic. It was tied 17–17 at the end of regulation. After 77 minutes and 54 seconds— the longest game in pro football history at the time—Dallas won on Tommy Brooker's field goal.

Despite winning the AFL championship, Hunt moved the Texans to Kansas City the following season. They renamed

Len Dawson holds the NFL record for most fumbles in a game. He coughed up the ball seven times against the San Diego Chargers on November 15, 1964.

Coach Hank Stram and quarterback Len Dawson led the Chiefs to Super Bowl IV.

Defensive back Fred Williamson called himself "The Hammer" for his bone-jarring tackles. Williamson went on to have a prolific acting career and was in the movie version of M*A*S*H.

themselves the Chiefs after Kansas City Mayor H. Roe Bartle. His nickname was "Chief."

The Chiefs had a brilliant coach, Hank Stram, and a terrific quarterback in Dawson. In 1966, Dawson led the AFL with 26 touchdown passes. His favorite target was Otis Taylor, a tall, physical receiver who averaged a league-best 22.4 yards per catch. Kansas City won its second AFL championship that year, easily beating the Buffalo Bills in the title game, 31–7.

That season, the AFL and NFL champions played each other for the first time in the AFL-NFL World Championship Game. It is now known as the Super Bowl. The **inaugural** game matched the Chiefs against the NFL's Green Bay Packers. The two teams met at the Los Angeles Coliseum on January 15, 1967. Kansas City trailed 14–10 at halftime, then fell apart in the second half and lost 35–10.

Two seasons later, the Chiefs relied primarily on their defense in posting a 12–2 record. They featured future Hall of Famers such as nose tackle Curley Culp, defensive tackle Buck Buchanan, and linebackers Bobby Bell and Willie Lanier. Together, they allowed an AFL record-low 170 points all season. The Chiefs lost in the playoffs, though, to the Oakland Raiders.

In 1969, Kansas City put it all together. Again, the rugged defense allowed the fewest points (177) in the league. The Chiefs finished 11–3, second to Oakland in the West. In the playoffs, they beat the defending Super Bowl champion New York Jets, 13–6. In that game, the defense staged a famous goal-line stand. They rose up to stop the Jets on three straight plays inside the one-yard line. The following weekend, the Chiefs beat Oakland, 17–7, in what was the final AFL Championship Game. Kansas City then won its first and only Super Bowl. Dawson led the Chiefs to a 23–7 victory over the Minnesota Vikings in Super Bowl IV.

Two seasons later, the Chiefs won the AFC West with a 10–3–1 record. On Christmas Day 1971, they hosted the Miami Dolphins in an AFC Divisional Playoff Game.

The Chiefs' victory over Minnesota in Super Bowl IV marked the last game played by an AFL team. The AFL–NFL merger took effect the following season.

Arrowhead Stadium is always a sea of red for Chiefs games.

The longest game in NFL history—Miami's victory over Kansas City in the 1971 playoffs—was the last game played at Municipal Stadium. The Chiefs moved into Arrowhead Stadium in 1972.

The game not only went into overtime, but it became the longest game in NFL history. Miami won, 27–24, when Garo Yepremian kicked the winning field goal in the marathon's 83rd minute.

Except for Kansas City's move into Arrowhead Stadium in 1972, the rest of the 1970s was forgettable. After 1973, Kansas City would not have another winning season until 1981.

In 1986, the Chiefs returned to the postseason

for the first time in 15 years. They lost their playoff opener to the Jets, though, 35–15. In 1989, super-sized fullback Christian Okoye, also known as the "Nigerian Nightmare," became the league's most feared rusher. Okoye steamrollered defenders en route to an NFL-best 1,480 rushing yards.

The Chiefs returned to the playoffs in 1990, spearheaded by an outstanding defense. End Neil Smith and linebacker Derrick Thomas led a unit that

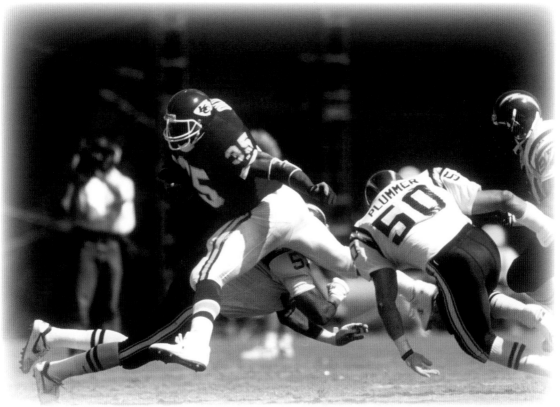

Christian Okoye was a nightmare for opposing defenses to tackle.

Derrick Thomas was one of the NFL's hardest-hitting tacklers.

Kansas City has never had an NFL MVP. Three players won MVPs before or after playing for the Chiefs: running back Marcus Allen and quarterbacks Joe Montana and Rich Gannon.

accounted for 60 sacks and 45 turnovers. Thomas had 20 sacks, including an NFL-record seven in one game.

Kansas City lost in the first round to Miami, however. Led by coach Marty Schottenheimer, the Chiefs would return to the playoffs each of the next five years. However, they never made it back to the Super Bowl. The toughest season was 1995, when Kansas City finished with a league-best 13–3 record.

Legendary quarterback Joe Montana joined Kansas City in the mid-1990s
and nearly got the Chiefs to the Super Bowl.

Chiefs running back Priest Holmes set an NFL record when he scored 27 touchdowns in 2003 (he broke the previous mark of 26 by St. Louis' Marshall Faulk in 2000).

However, they were upset at home in the playoffs by the Indianapolis Colts. The Chiefs were 13–3 again two years later, only to lose to the Broncos in the playoffs.

In January 2000, the Chiefs were devastated when Thomas—Kansas City's best and most popular player—died of injuries he received in a car accident.

The Chiefs eventually missed the playoffs for the fourth consecutive year the following season, but in 2001 Kansas City's hopes were restored by the hiring of Dick Vermeil as head coach.

Vermeil, who had been out of coaching for one season after leading the St. Louis Rams to victory in Super Bowl XXXIV, immediately began molding the Chiefs into a contender. By 2002, he had built the NFL's highest-scoring offense around star running back Priest Holmes, quarterback Trent Green, and tight end Tony Gonzalez. One year later, the Chiefs won 13 regular-season games and the AFC West title, and reached the playoffs for the first time since the 1997 season. They averaged 30.3 points per game that year while scoring 484 points, the most in the NFL.

Running back Priest Holmes has been the key cog in the Chiefs'
high-flying offense the past several seasons.

CHAPTER THREE

THE OAKLAND RAIDERS

If Darth Vader had a favorite football team, it would be the Oakland Raiders. Like Lord Vader, the Raiders wear black and embrace the role of the villain. Former stars include players nick-named Ghost, Snake, and Assassin. No professional sports franchise has a bigger reputation for scaring opponents.

The Silver and Black, as the Raiders are often called after their team colors, was founded in 1960. The franchise's low point came in 1962. Oakland lost its first 13 games that season, after having lost its final six games of the 1961 season.

Raiders' history reversed itself on January 15, 1963. Oakland hired Al Davis, a young assistant coach with the San Diego Chargers, as its head coach and general manager. "We started doing things first class instead of third class," said former Raiders center Jim Otto. Otto was a fixture on the offensive line for the franchise's first 15 seasons.

Famed for wearing number 00, Otto was the foundation. Soon, Davis added other all-stars such

George Blanda, who spent the final nine of his 26 pro seasons with Oakland, owns six NFL career records, including most seasons (26) and most games played (340).

Daryle Lamonica's long passes earned him the nickname "Mad Bomber."

as wide receiver Fred Biletnikoff and quarterback and kicker George Blanda.

Five years after finishing 1–13, Oakland went 13–1 in 1967. Quarterback Daryle Lamonica was named AFL MVP, and the Raiders crushed the Houston Oilers, 40–7, in the championship game. Oakland met the Green Bay Packers in Super Bowl II, but lost, 33–14.

The Raiders won 25 postseason games in their history through 2004. Only the Cowboys, with 32, had more (the 49ers also were at 25).

Raiders' defenders chase New York Jets quarterback Joe Namath during the famous "Heidi Game" in 1968. Oakland won in the last minute, 43–32.

In 1968, the Raiders were involved in one of the most famous games in NFL history. Oakland trailed the visiting New York Jets 32–29 with just over a minute to play in a nationally televised game. Suddenly, the clock struck 7 P.M. NBC switched from the game to its regularly scheduled program, the film *Heidi.* Thousands of angry football fans called to complain. They all missed an amazing ending to a wild game. In the final minute, Oakland scored a pair of touchdowns to win, 43–32.

Four years later, Oakland, then coached by John Madden, visited the Pittsburgh Steelers in a divisional

The Raiders couldn't stop Franco Harris during the "Immaculate Reception" in 1972.

Ken Stabler was poised and efficient as Oakland's quarterback for much of the 1970s.

Al Davis's motto during the Raiders' 1980 Super Bowl season was, "Just win, baby." It has become the team's signature.

playoff game. The contest was decided by one of the most famous plays in NFL playoff history, the "Immaculate Reception."

Only 22 seconds remained. Oakland led 7–6. Pittsburgh faced fourth down and 10 with the ball on its own 40. Steelers quarterback Terry Bradshaw heaved a pass to running back Frenchy Fuqua. Raiders safety Jack Tatum, nicknamed "Assassin" for his bone-rattling hits, collided with Fuqua as the ball arrived. The football ricocheted into the arms of Steelers running back Franco Harris. Harris caught the ball just above his shoelaces and rambled 42 yards for the winning touchdown.

In 1976, the Raiders won the AFC West for the ninth time in 10 seasons. The 13–1 squad was filled with free-spirited legends. Five players from the team would eventually make the Pro Football Hall of Fame. They included tight end Dave Casper ("Ghost") and Biletnikoff. Others on their way to the Hall were offensive linemen Art Shell and Gene Upshaw. Ray Guy became the only punter elected to the Hall.

Oakland, which had lost the last three AFC Championship Games, finally made it back to the Super Bowl by trouncing Pittsburgh in the conference title game. Then the Silver and Black manhandled the Minnesota Vikings, 32–14, in Super Bowl XI.

In 1978, the Raiders forced an NFL rule change following a 21–20 win at San Diego. Oakland trailed 20–14 in the final seconds. A moment before being sacked, Stabler purposely fumbled the ball forward. Another player intentionally batted the ball toward the end zone. Casper fell on it there for the game-winning touchdown. After that, the league added a new rule. Now, only the player who fumbles the ball on fourth down or in the final two minutes can advance it.

Madden retired after the 1978 season and launched a career as a top football TV announcer. However, the Raiders remained successful. Quarterback Jim Plunkett, a former Heisman Trophy winner, was

The "Ghost to the Post" was Dave Casper's 42-yard catch that set up the tying field goal late in regulation of the Raiders' victory over the Colts in the 1977 playoffs.

Running back Marcus Allen and the Raiders were number one after winning Super Bowl XVIII.

The Raiders were the kings of Monday night in the 1970s and 1980s. From 1975 to 1981, they won 14 consecutive games on *Monday Night Football.*

the MVP of Oakland's 27–10 victory over Philadelphia in Super Bowl XV to cap the 1980 season. Three years later, running back Marcus Allen, another former Heisman winner, led the Raiders to a 38–9 rout of Washington in Super Bowl XVIII.

By that time, the Raiders were in Los Angeles. In 1982, Davis, now the Raiders' owner, had moved the team. The Raiders remained in Southern California for 13 seasons. The highlights of the Los Angeles era included the hiring of Art Shell as head coach in 1989. The former tackle became the NFL's first African American head coach since Fritz Pollard in 1920.

The Raiders returned to Oakland in 1995. In the 2001 postseason, they lost a heartbreaking divisional playoff game at New England. Patriots quarterback Tom Brady appeared to lose a fumble late in the game, clinching the win for Oakland. The officials over-ruled themselves in the snowy night, however. Their ruling gave New England another chance. The Patriots eventually won the game and, two weeks later, Super Bowl XXXVI.

In 2002, the Raiders returned to AFC supremacy. They finished with the conference's best record at 11–5. Veteran quarterback Rich Gannon was the league's MVP. He guided a powerful offense that also featured future Hall of Fame wide receivers Tim Brown and Jerry Rice. In the playoffs, Oakland easily dispatched the Jets and the Titans to win the conference title. Though the Raiders lost Super Bowl XXXVII to the Buccaneers, the Silver and Black had proved it was back.

Unfortunately, the Raiders' return to the top did not last long. One year after winning the AFC championship, Oakland tumbled to a 4–12 mark in 2003 (equaling the poorest in the NFL). Head coach Bill Callahan was replaced by Norv Turner the following season, but the Raiders' fortunes improved only slightly. They won only five games and finished in last place in the AFC West.

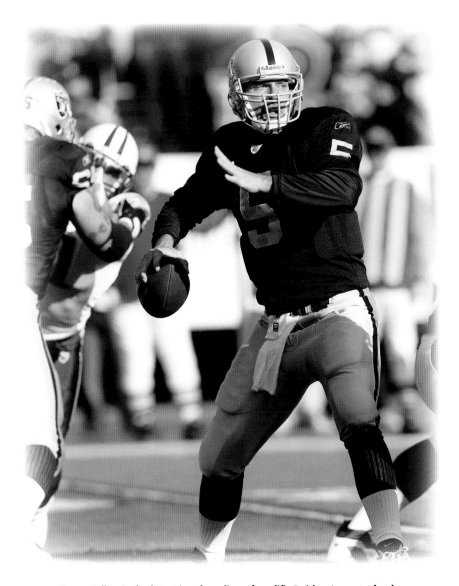

Kerry Collins is the latest in a long line of prolific Raiders' quarterbacks.

One bright spot was the play of quarterback Kerry Collins, a free-agent signee. Collins, the man who helped lead the New York Giants to Super Bowl XXXV in the 2000 season, replaced the injured Gannon early in the year. Despite starting only 13 games, he passed for 3,495 yards and 21 touchdowns.

CHAPTER FOUR

THE SAN DIEGO CHARGERS

From the moment the Chargers placed lightning bolts on their helmets, no other pro football franchise has provided more jolts of offensive electricity. If the old AFL was known for having wide-open, high-scoring contests, then San Diego was its poster boy.

The franchise was originally the Los Angeles Chargers. Barron Hilton, the hotel **magnate,** was the owner. He liked the name Chargers because it symbolized electricity as well as his hotel chain's new credit card.

Sid Gillman, who is to the exciting offense what Thomas Edison was to the light bulb, was the Chargers' first coach. Talk about electric: On the team's first play in its first preseason game, Paul Lowe returned a kickoff 105 yards for a touchdown.

The Chargers won the AFL West their first year, 1960, with a 10-4 record. They averaged 26.6 points per game. Quarterback Jack Kemp, an NFL reject, was rated the league's best passer. In the first

In 1980, San Diego Stadium was renamed Jack Murphy Stadium in honor of the late sports editor of the *San Diego Union.* In the late 1990s, it was re-renamed Qualcomm Stadium after a deal with a communications company.

Chrysler officials unveiled the company's new automobile, the "Charger," at halftime of San Diego's loss to Buffalo in the 1965 AFL title game.

AFL Championship Game, Los Angeles lost to the Houston Oilers, 24–16.

The following season, the Chargers moved to San Diego. They went 12–2 but again lost to Houston in the championship game.

After their first losing season in 1962, San Diego made three straight trips to the AFL Championship Game. In 1963, the Chargers routed the Boston Patriots, 51–10, to win their first, and only, title. They lost the championship game to the Buffalo Bills in each of the next two seasons. Adding insult to injury, the quarterback of those Bills' squads was Kemp. The Chargers had tried to sneak Kemp through **waivers** during the 1962 preseason. Buffalo claimed him for $100.

Lance Alworth was the Chargers' star. Nicknamed "Bambi" because of his slight build and nimble grace, Alworth averaged 100 receiving yards per game for three straight seasons (1964–1966). Alworth's elusiveness and sure hands made him unforgettable. In 1978, he became the first AFL player enshrined in the Pro Football Hall of Fame.

Alworth's enshrinement must have energized the Chargers. The franchise had failed to finish better than third place from 1966 to 1978, but suddenly San Diego's offense reacted as if it had been struck by lightning. Actually, the **catalyst** was head coach Don Coryell, who was hired in 1978. Coryell had the most inventive offensive mind pro football had seen since Gillman.

The new coach's offense was known as "Air Coryell." His primary weapons were quarterback Dan Fouts and tight end Kellen

Lance Alworth's great skills earned him a spot in the Pro Football Hall of Fame.

Winslow, who were both future Hall of Famers. Wide receivers John Jefferson and Charlie Joiner also were potent and prolific.

In 1979, Fouts had four consecutive 300-yard games (a record) and passed for 4,082 yards (another record). At 12–4, the Chargers were not only winners, but they were also tremendous fun to watch.

San Diego lost its playoff opener in 1979 to Houston, 17–14. But Air Coryell returned in 1980 and soared even higher. Fouts passed for 4,715 yards and his trio of receivers each had 1,000-yard seasons. The

Chargers defensive back Vencie Glenn recorded the longest interception return in NFL history against the Denver Broncos in 1987. He raced 103 yards for a touchdown after intercepting the Broncos' John Elway in the end zone.

Chargers beat Buffalo 20–14 in the first round of the playoffs, their first postseason victory since 1963. The following weekend they lost to Oakland, 34–27, in the AFC Championship Game.

In 1981, the Chargers won the AFC West a third straight time. Fouts again shattered the pass-

Dan Fouts is among the most successful NFL passers ever.

Tight end Kellen Winslow had to be helped off the field after his exhausting performance in a dramatic 1982 playoff game.

ing yardage barrier with 4,802. Winslow led the AFC in receptions for the second year in a row. It was all prelude to one of the most memorable postseason games ever.

On January 2, 1982, the Chargers traveled to Miami to face the Dolphins in a divisional playoff. San Diego led 24–0 after one quarter. But Miami came back, and the teams were tied 38–38 after four quarters. In overtime, Winslow blocked a field-goal

The Chargers reached Super Bowl XXIX when linebacker Dennis Gibson knocked down a pass at the goal line to preserve a victory over Pittsburgh in the AFC title game.

37

**Burly running back Natrone Means helped carry San Diego
to Super Bowl XXIX, though the Chargers lost to the 49ers.**

try. Finally, after 13:52 of overtime, the Chargers' Rolf Benirschke made the game-winning field goal.

In 1995, his rookie season, Chargers punter Darren Bennett became the first Australian-born player to play in the Pro Bowl.

The Chargers' glory was short-lived. Eight days later, the temperature in Cincinnati was 11 degrees below zero, a far cry from the balmy climes of San Diego. The Chargers lost, 27–7, and would not return to the playoffs for 10 years.

The drought ended in 1992. The new-look Chargers relied on defensive stoppers such as end Leslie O'Neal and middle linebacker Junior Seau (pronounced "Say Ow!") to win the AFC West.

Two years later, the Chargers advanced all the way to the Super Bowl. Burly fullback Natrone Means gained a franchise-record 1,350 yards. Head coach Bobby Ross put together a defense that stuffed opponents. That is, until

In 2004, second-year star Antonio Gates caught more touchdown passes (13) than any other tight end in NFL history.

Super Bowl XXIX, where the San Francisco 49ers won easily, 49–26.

Ross resigned a few seasons later, and the Chargers entered a prolonged period of decline. In 2000, San Diego tied an NFL record for futility by losing 15 games.

The silver lining to that dark cloud, however, came in the 2001 draft. Because the Chargers had the league's poorest record, they owned the top selection. Superstar quarterback Michael Vick was available, but San Diego traded the choice. And though the Chargers were criticized for the move, it enabled them to come away with two excellent players instead of one: quarterback Drew Brees and running back LaDainian Tomlinson.

Tomlinson was an immediate star and set a franchise record by running for 1,683 yards in 2002. The next year, he set another record by catching 100 passes. Brees took a little longer to develop, but he had a breakout season in 2004, when he passed for 3,159 yards and 27 touchdowns.

That year, San Diego won 12 games and made the playoffs for the first time since 1995. Brees was named the NFL's comeback player of the year (he had passed for just 2,108 yards and 11 touchdowns the season before) and Marty Schottenheimer, who had been hired in 2002, was named the coach of the year.

Though the season ended with a heartbreaking loss to the New York Jets in overtime in the first round, the Chargers gave their fans a memorable year—and newfound hopes for a bright future.

LaDainian Tomlinson is one of the NFL's superstar running backs.

STAT STUFF

TEAM RECORDS

TEAM	ALL-TIME RECORD	NFL TITLES (MOST RECENT)	NUMBER OF TIMES IN PLAYOFFS	TOP COACH (WINS)
Denver	349–317–10	2 (1998)	16	Dan Reeves (117)
Kansas City	356–308–12	1 (1969)	14	Hank Stram (129)
Oakland	390–275–11	4 (1983)	21	John Madden (112)
San Diego	320–345–11	1 (1963)	13	Sid Gillman (83)

MEMBERS OF THE PRO FOOTBALL HALL OF FAME

DENVER PLAYER	POSITION	DATE INDUCTED
Willie Brown	Cornerback	1984
Tony Dorsett	Running Back	1994
John Elway	Quarterback	2004

KANSAS CITY PLAYER	POSITION	DATE INDUCTED
Marcus Allen	Running Back	2003
Bobby Bell	Linebacker/Defensive End	1983
Junious (Buck) Buchanan	Defensive Tackle	1990
Len Dawson	Quarterback	1987
Lamar Hunt	Owner	1972
Willie Lanier	Linebacker	1986
Marv Levy	Coach	2001
Joe Montana	Quarterback	2002
Jan Stenerud	Kicker	1991
Hank Stram	Coach	2003
Mike Webster	Center	1997

MORE STAT STUFF

M E M B E R S   O F   T H E   P R O   F O O T B A L L   H A L L   O F   F A M E

OAKLAND PLAYER	POSITION	DATE INDUCTED
Marcus Allen	Running Back	2003
Fred Biletnikoff	Wide Receiver	1988
George Blanda	Quarterback/Kicker	1981
Bob Brown	Tackle	2004
Willie Brown	Cornerback	1984
Dave Casper	Tight End	2002
Al Davis	Owner/Coach	1992
Eric Dickerson	Running Back	1999
Mike Haynes	Cornerback	1997
Ted Hendricks	Linebacker	1990
James Lofton	Wide Receiver	2003
Howie Long	Defensive End	2000
Ronnie Lott	Cornerback/Safety	2000
Ron Mix	Offensive Tackle	1979
Jim Otto	Center	1980
Art Shell	Tackle	1989
Gene Upshaw	Guard	1987

SAN DIEGO PLAYER	POSITION	DATE INDUCTED
Lance Alworth	Flanker	1978
Dan Fouts	Quarterback	1993
Sid Gillman	Coach	1983
Charlie Joiner	Wide Receiver	1996
David (Deacon) Jones	Defensive End	1980
Larry Little	Guard	1993
John Mackey	Tight End	1992
Ron Mix	Tackle	1979
Johnny Unitas	Quarterback	1979
Kellen Winslow	Tight End	1995

MORE STAT STUFF

43

MORE STAT STUFF

A F C   W E S T   C A R E E R   L E A D E R S   (T H R O U G H   2 0 0 4)

DENVER

CATEGORY	NAME (YEARS WITH TEAM)	TOTAL
Rushing yards	Terrell Davis (1995-2002)	7,607
Passing yards	John Elway (1983-1998)	51,475
Touchdown passes	John Elway (1983-1998)	300
Receptions	Rod Smith (1995-2004)	712
Touchdowns	Terrell Davis (1995-2002)	65
Scoring	Jason Elam (1993-2004)	1,457

KANSAS CITY

CATEGORY	NAME (YEARS WITH TEAM)	TOTAL
Rushing yards	Priest Holmes (2001-04)	5,482
Passing yards	Len Dawson (1962-1975)	28,507
Touchdown passes	Len Dawson (1962-1975)	237
Receptions	Tony Gonzalez (1997-2004)	570
Touchdowns	Priest Holmes (2001-04)	70
Scoring	Nick Lowery (1980-1993)	1,466

OAKLAND

CATEGORY	NAME (YEARS WITH TEAM)	TOTAL
Rushing yards	Marcus Allen (1982-1992)	8,545
Passing yards	Ken Stabler (1970-79)	19,078
Touchdown passes	Ken Stabler (1970-79)	150
Receptions	Tim Brown (1988-2003)	1,070
Touchdowns	Tim Brown (1988-2003)	14,734
Scoring	George Blanda (1967-1975)	863

SAN DIEGO

CATEGORY	NAME (YEARS WITH TEAM)	TOTAL
Rushing yards	LaDainian Tomlinson (2001-04)	5,899
Passing yards	Dan Fouts (1973-1987)	43,040
Touchdown passes	Dan Fouts (1973-1987)	254
Receptions	Charlie Joiner (1976-1986)	586
Touchdowns	Lance Alworth (1962-1970)	83
Scoring	John Carney (1990-2000)	1,076

GLOSSARY

bona fide—authentic or genuine; real

catalyst—the person or thing that instigates change

cornerstone—a vital or fundamental part of something

expansion team—a new franchise that starts from scratch

inaugural—the first one

magnate—a powerful or influential businessperson

sacked—when a quarterback is tackled behind the line of scrimmage while attempting to pass

Super Bowl—the NFL's annual championship game, played in late January or early February at a different stadium each year

turnovers—when teams give up possession of the ball by throwing interceptions or losing fumbles

waivers—when teams give up their rights to players, allowing other teams to sign them

TIME LINE

1960 The Dallas Texans, Denver Broncos, Los Angeles Chargers, and Oakland Raiders become charter members of the American Football League

1961 The Chargers move their franchise to San Diego

1963 The Texans move to Kansas City and become the Chiefs

1963 San Diego wins its first, and only, league championship

1966 Kansas City wins the AFL title and plays in the first Super Bowl

1969 The Chiefs win the last Super Bowl before the AFL-NFL merger, beating Minnesota

1976 The Raiders beat the Vikings for the first of the franchise's three Super Bowl victories

1977 Denver makes the playoffs for the first time in franchise history, but loses Super Bowl XII to Dallas

1982 Oakland shifts its franchise to Los Angeles

1994 San Diego reaches the Super Bowl for the first time, but loses game XXIX to San Francisco

1995 The Raiders move back to Oakland

1997 After four losses in the Super Bowl, the Broncos win the first of back-to-back titles

FOR MORE INFORMATION ABOUT

THE AFC WEST AND THE NFL

BOOKS

Buckley, James Jr., and Jerry Rice. *America's Greatest Game.* New York: Hyperion Books for Children, 1998.

Elway, John. *Comeback Kid.* Dallas: Taylor Publishing, 1997.

Frisch, Aaron. *The History of the Oakland Raiders.* Mankato, Minn.: Creative Eduction, 2005.

Hawkes, Brian. *The History of the Kansas City Chiefs.* Mankato, Minn.: Creative Eduction, 2005.

Schmalzbauer, Adam. *The History of the Denver Broncos.* Mankato, Minn.: Creative Eduction, 2005.

Schmalzbauer, Adam. *The History of the San Diego Chargers.* Mankato, Minn.: Creative Eduction, 2005.

ON THE WEB

Visit our home page for lots of links about the AFC West:

http://www.childsworld.com/links

Note to Parents, Teachers, and Librarians: We routinely verify our Web links to make sure they are safe, active sites—so encourage your readers to check them out!

INDEX

A B O U T   T H E   A U T H O R

John Walters is a former staff writer at *Sports Illustrated* who worked at the magazine from 1989 to 2001. He has also written two books, *Basketball for Dummies,* which he co-wrote with former Notre Dame basketball coach Digger Phelps, and *The Same River Twice: A Season with Geno Auriemma and the Connecticut Huskies,* which chronicles the women's basketball team's 2000–2001 season.